# CONTENTS

KU-092-613

The Hubble Space Telescope orbits around the Earth. It was placed in this path by the space shuttle *Discovery* on 25 April 1990.

EDGE
BOOKS

# SPACE

## FACTS OR FIBS

KRISTIN J. RUSSO

Raintree is an imprint of Capstone Global Library Limited, a company incorporated in England and Wales having its registered office at 264 Banbury Road, Oxford, OX2 7DY – Registered company number: 6695582

www.raintree.co.uk
myorders@raintree.co.uk

Edited by Lauren Dupuis-Perez
Designed by Sara Radka
Production by Laura Manthe

ISBN 978 1 4747 5453 8
22 21 20 19 18
10 9 8 7 6 5 4 3 2 1

British Library Cataloguing in Publication Data
A full catalogue record for this book is available from the British Library.

**Acknowledgements**
Getty Images: adventtr, 6, Bill Ingalls/NASA, 28 (top), Flickr RF, 13, 18, 21, iLexx, 24, Image Source, 15, JAXA/NASA/Hinode, 11, Marc Ward/Stocktrek Images, cover (astronaut), NASA, 29, Nerthuz, cover (telescope), Yayasya, 7, 19, 9 (bottom), ZargonDesign, 20, back cover; iStockphoto: den-belitsky, 14, scyther5, 17, sololos, background, cover (background); NASA: 4, 8, 12, 16, 22, 26, 27 (both), PL-Caltech, 23, SDO/AIA, 10; Newscom: Alex Milan Tracy/NurPhoto/ZUMAPRESS, 25, NASA/Sipa USA, 28 (bottom)

Graphic elements by Capstone Press and Book Buddy Media.

# PACE THROUGH TIME

Thousands of years ago, people made up stories to explain what they saw in the sky. Different groups had ideas about the sun, clouds, stars and moon. Ancient Egyptians believed in Re, the sun god. He had children with special powers. These children became the planet Earth, the stars, the **atmosphere** and the clouds. The Norse Vikings believed the sun and moon were pulled through the sky by chariots. The ancient Greeks believed in gods and goddesses. These beings controlled the sky. Later, the Greeks used maths to explain how the planets and stars moved in the sky. Many of their ideas helped scientists make new discoveries.

We no longer rely on myths and stories to help us understand space. Instead, we use scientific tools. Today, astronauts and scientists work together to improve space exploration. They use telescopes and **satellites** to learn more than ever before about our **solar system**.

People used to believe Earth was flat, but now we know that is not true. People also used to think Earth was the centre of the solar system. This is also not true. Today, scientists know a lot more about space than people did in the past. But they are still trying to figure out what is a fact and what is a fib when it comes to outer space.

**atmosphere** layer of gases that surrounds some planets, dwarf planets and moons
**satellite** spacecraft that circles Earth; satellites gather and send information to Earth
**solar system** sun and the objects that move around it

# CHAPTER 1

# PLANETS

The sun is the centre of the solar system. It takes eight minutes for light to travel from the sun to Earth.

People used to believe the sun circled around Earth. Scientists proved this to be false. Earth and all of the planets in our solar system travel around the sun. Scientists know that discovering new facts can take time. For example, researchers are searching for more planets in our solar system. They have watched the sky closely to learn how the solar system works. The solar system includes the sun and all of the planets that revolve around it.

**IT'S TRUE!** Mercury and Earth move at different speeds. When Mercury appears to move backwards, we say it is "in retrograde". There is no scientific proof that this affects Earth. Some people believe that crazy things happen when Mercury is in retrograde. They blame accidents and communication mix-ups on the position of the planets.

# There are nine planets in our solar system.

## Evidence

There are several requirements that must be met before something can be considered a planet. First, a planet must travel around the sun. It must have a nearly round shape. The planet's gravity must be strong enough to push other celestial bodies out of its path. It can also pull them in to make them part of the planet. For 70 years, scientists agreed that there were nine planets in the solar system.

## Answer: UNDECIDED

In 2006 scientists decided that Pluto is not an official planet. It does not meet all the requirements. It is now called a "dwarf planet".

Today, there are eight official planets. They are Mercury, Venus, Earth, Mars, Jupiter, Saturn, Uranus and Neptune. But there may be one more.

In January 2015, **astronomers** announced that they had discovered another possible planet. It is called Planet Nine. Planet Nine is far away from the sun. It would take about 10,000 to 20,000 years to complete its **orbit**. If scientists agree, Planet Nine could become an official planet. This would raise the number of planets in our solar system to nine.

**astronomer**  scientist who studies stars, planets and other objects in space
**orbit**  path an object follows as it goes around the sun or a planet

# FACT OR FIB?

Except for the sun and the moon, the International Space Station (ISS) is the brightest object in the sky.

The ISS moves so quickly that it could go to the moon and back in one day. The ISS sees an average of 16 sunrises and sunsets every 24 hours.

The ISS is a large spacecraft. Astronauts can live there and work in space. Astronauts from many different countries share missions at the ISS.

**International Space Station (ISS)** large spacecraft where astronauts live and work in space

8

## Evidence

There are large, gold-coloured solar panels on the ISS. Solar panels use energy from the sun to generate electricity. The solar panels are powerful. They reflect so much light, they make the ISS appear as bright as Venus in the night sky.

## Answer: FACT

In 2009 **NASA** attached new solar panels. These new panels mean that the ISS can harness even more energy from the sun. They also reflect more sunlight, enough to make the ISS the third-brightest object in the sky. It is also the brightest man-made object in the sky.

 **IT'S TRUE!** The Hubble Space Telescope is named for Edwin Powell Hubble. He discovered the existence of other galaxies. The telescope was launched into space in 1990. This strong telescope orbits Earth and gives scientists a detailed view of the universe.

**NASA** US government agency that does research on flight and space exploration; NASA stands for National Aeronautics and Space Administration

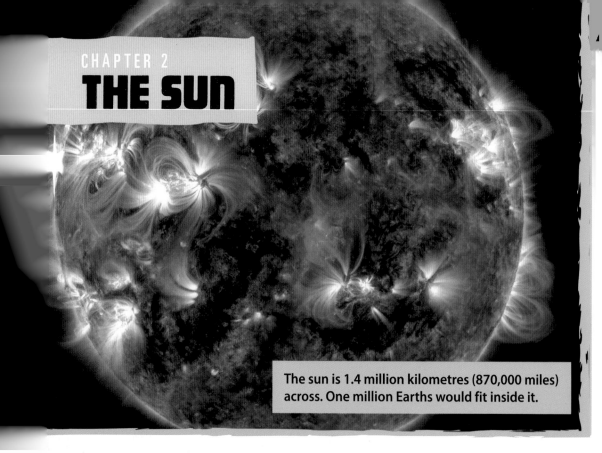

# CHAPTER 2
# THE SUN

The sun is 1.4 million kilometres (870,000 miles) across. One million Earths would fit inside it.

The sun is a powerful star. It has been shining for about 4.6 billion years. Without its warmth and energy, there would be no life on Earth. Scientists think the sun will burn for 5 billion more years. Then the sun could burn out. It will take about 1 trillion years to fully cool off.

In the daytime, the sun is far too bright for people to look at directly. The sun's brightness will cause eye pain and damage. During a solar **eclipse**, the sun's light is blocked.

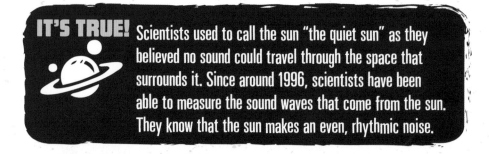

**IT'S TRUE!** Scientists used to call the sun "the quiet sun" as they believed no sound could travel through the space that surrounds it. Since around 1996, scientists have been able to measure the sound waves that come from the sun. They know that the sun makes an even, rhythmic noise.

People should not look directly at the sun during an **eclipse.**

## Evidence

During a solar eclipse, the moon moves between the sun and Earth. The moon blocks part of the sun's light. A solar eclipse is rare. It can only be seen from certain spots on Earth. Sometimes it happens only once in a person's lifetime. Solar eclipses are special events. People want to make sure they have the chance to see them.

## Answer: FACT

Looking at the sun is harmful at all times. Not many people stare at the sun long enough to go completely blind. But sometimes the damage to their eyes can be permanent. According to NASA, the only safe way to view an eclipse is to use sun filters, special goggles or pinhole viewers.

. . . . . . . . . . . . . . . . . . . . . . . . . . . . . . . . . . . .

**eclipse**  when one object in space blocks light and stops it shining on another object in space

The sun is nearly 150 million km (93 million miles) away from Earth. The surface of the sun looks calm and peaceful. Scientists know that this is not true. The outer layer of the sun bubbles. It has hot gases and **plasma**. Scientists study the sun to see if it can affect people living on Earth.

**FACT OR FIB?**

## Space weather on the sun is too far away to affect Earth.

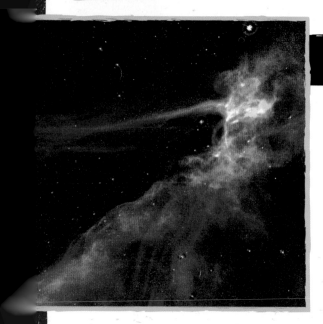

## Evidence

The sun is powerful. It releases a constant stream of particles into space. This is called the solar wind. It is what pushes a comet's atmosphere out into a tail shape. The solar wind travels up to 3 million km (1.9 million miles) per hour.

**IT'S TRUE!**

So far, astronomers have found about 500 other solar systems in our galaxy, which is called the Milky Way. There are probably millions more. Researchers believe there are sun-like stars in these other solar systems.

Particles from the sun carried by the solar wind can make particles in our atmosphere glow. This creates an aurora, also called the northern lights or southern lights.

## Answer: FIB

Strong, powerful weather from the sun's surface can affect Earth. It can disturb electric and magnetic fields on Earth. Extreme space weather disrupts our communication systems.

On 2 September 1859, space weather interrupted telegraph services. The telegraph was used to send messages before the telephone. In 1989, severe space weather caused a transformer failure on Earth. Transformers convert high levels of energy into lower levels of energy. This created a **blackout** that lasted more than nine hours and affected more than 6 million people.

Today, scientists worry that space weather caused by the sun will affect communication on aeroplanes. Aeroplanes are designed so that they do not have to rely on satellite communication to land safely.

**plasma** matter that is a collection of hot, charged atoms, such as those found in a fluorescent light bulb, neon sign or star

**blackout** period of darkness caused by power failure

# CHAPTER 3
# STARS

Observing the night sky is possible even without help from binoculars or telescopes. Five planets – Mercury, Venus, Mars, Jupiter and Saturn – are all visible to the naked eye.

For thousands of years, people have looked to the stars when they were lost. The North Star helped people find true north. Once they knew which direction was north, they could work out how to find south, east and west. Travellers and explorers still rely on stars and **constellations** to help them with direction. They can also use the sun to track time.

**IT'S TRUE!** Do you know how to tell the difference between a star and a planet? Stars twinkle, while planets and moons have a steady shine.

# Stars can be used to help people track time.

## Evidence

Because Earth spins, the stars seem to move. They are actually fixed in the night sky. This means stars and constellations can be tracked by people on Earth. Astronomers also use stars and constellations to measure distances to other stars and galaxies.

## Answer: FACT

Most nations today use the **Gregorian calendar**. The calendar uses the sun and the moon to keep track of days and months. The Gregorian calendar uses the 12-month, 24-hour-day system. Most countries use this calendar.

Astronomers use a different method of tracking time. This system is called the Julian Day system. It counts the days since 4713 BC. The Julian Day system is the official time recording system for scientists who study outer space and is based on star movement. Computer programmes keep track of information about stars using the Julian Day system.

The US Naval Observatory has posted an online converter so people can work out what day it is according to the Julian Day system. For example, 10 May 2017, is actually 2457883.5 in the Julian Day system.

**constellation** group of stars that appear to form a shape
**Gregorian calendar** calendar used by much of the world; it was established in 1582 by Pope Gregory XIII

Stars burn for billions of years, but eventually, they run out of fuel. Depending on the type of star that is dying, the results can be dramatic. Some dying stars explode, leaving behind a black hole. Others swell up and shed their outer layers to form a ring. Finally, the center will cool into a white dwarf and then eventually into a black dwarf. This entire process takes a few billion years.

## FACT OR FIB?

# When a star dies, it is no longer visible.

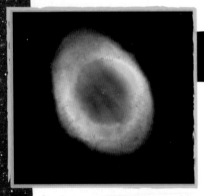

## Evidence

When the force of a star's collapse is very great, a black hole is sometimes created. Black holes are areas where no light can escape. When gas moves around the black hole it can become very hot. This heat sends **x-rays** out into space.

## Answer: FIB

It takes billions of years for a star to complete the dying process. During that time, light from the dying star travels to and is visible from Earth. Light travels quickly, but it still takes time. Some of the stars we still see in the sky today died tens of thousands of years ago. The light created from when they burned out is still traveling to Earth.

• • • • • • • • • • • • • • • • • • • • • • • • • • • • • • • • • • • • •

**x-ray** powerful invisible ray that can pass through various objects

The most famous black hole is Cygnus X-1. It was found inside the constellation of Cygnus the swan in 1972.

**IT'S TRUE!** A falling star, which is also called a shooting star, is not actually a star. The streaks of light that are called shooting stars are actually bits of dust and rock that burn up when they fall into Earth's atmosphere.

# CHAPTER 4

# ASTEROIDS, METEORS AND COMETS

WIth its long, bright tails streaming out, Comet McNaught appeared in the sky in 2007.

**Asteroids** and comets are large chunks of rock and ice in space. Scientists believe they formed at the same time the planets formed. Asteroids and comets were not absorbed into the forming planets. Meteors are pieces of rock that enter Earth's atmosphere. Once they enter Earth's atmosphere, they either burn up or land on Earth's surface. If they land on Earth, they become meteorites.

· · · · · · · · · · · · · · · · · · · · · · · · · · · · · · · · · · · · · · · · · · ·

**asteroid**  large space rock that moves around the sun

# FACT OR FIB?

## An asteroid or comet is on a collision course with Earth.

## Evidence

If an asteroid hit Earth, the explosion would cause debris to fly into the atmosphere. The debris would block sunlight. It would kill plant and animal life. Humans would be at risk.

Some scientists believe that an asteroid hitting Earth caused the **mass extinction** that killed the dinosaurs. Others believe that craters are evidence that asteroids have hit Earth in the past. There is a crater near the Grand Canyon in Arizona, USA.

Scientist know that asteroids do hit planets. They can cause serious damage. Scientists believe that Uranus orbits on its side because it was hit with asteroids. These hits were so powerful, they caused the planet to tilt.

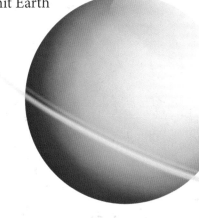

**IT'S TRUE!** Comets are called "dirty snowballs" because they are made of rock, dust, ice and frozen gases. Some scientists think that comets brought water to Earth when the solar system was first created.

**mass extinction** widespread and rapid decrease in life on Earth

# Answer: FIB

There are many asteroids, comets and meteoroids flying through space. Scientists use modern technology to track these objects. There is an asteroid known as 2002 NT7. It has a very small chance of hitting Earth in 2019. Scientists are watching this asteroid closely. Research shows that this asteroid will most likely not hit Earth.

Scientists are also watching an asteroid named Bennu. It has a chance of hitting Earth in 2175. Current information indicates that there is no danger from an asteroid or any other object from space hitting Earth any time soon.

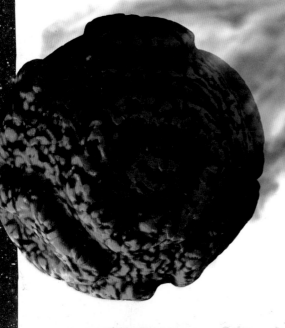

Smoke trails can be seen when a large meteorite crashes into Earth during the day.

**IT'S TRUE!** A meteor shower is a collection of so many meteors that it looks like they are raining down in the night sky. There are about 12 meteor showers each year.

During the Geminid meteor shower, you can see a falling meteor about once every minute. The Geminid meteor shower usually takes place each December.

# CHAPTER 5

# ALIENS AND UFOS

The Hubble Telescope has taken a picture in which 10,000 galaxies are visible. These are the spiralling galaxies NCG 2207 and IC 2163.

Scientists estimate that there are about 100 billion planets in the Milky Way. Scientists use the Hubble Telescope to see our galaxy. They think some planets may support life. Many of these planets orbit stars like our sun.

**IT'S TRUE!** The world's largest radio telescope is called FAST, which stands for Five-hundred-metre Aperture Spherical Telescope. It was built in China. It is large enough to cover the size of 30 football pitches. Russia and Puerto Rico also have enormous telescopes that rival China's FAST in size.

## FACT OR FIB?

**Scientists have found definitive evidence of life on other planets.**

## Evidence

Scientists are looking for signs of life on other planets. Pictures of Mars show that water sometimes flows on the surface of the planet. The Mars **rover** *Curiosity* climbed a Martian mountain. It found evidence of billion-year-old lakes. This is the type of environment that could support life forms. These life forms would be small. You would only be able to see them through a microscope.

## Answer: FIB

If life forms do exist on other planets in our solar system, no definitive proof has been found. Scientists have only found some conditions to support life. They are still searching for life itself.

**rover** small vehicle that people can move by using a remote control; rovers are used to explore objects in space

Astronomers have found about 500 solar systems in the Milky Way so far. Each year they discover new solar systems. They can even find new galaxies. There might be tens of billions of planets in our galaxy. There might be as many as 100 billion. It is possible that at least one other planet outside our solar system could support life. It is possible that these life forms could also travel in space.

# FACT OR FIB?

## Aliens have made contact with humans.

## Evidence

People have reported seeing unidentified flying objects (UFOs) in the sky. Many people wonder if UFOs are spaceships. They usually don't move like aeroplanes or helicopters. Sometimes UFOs flash bright colours. Sometimes they move very quickly. Many people believe that UFOs carry extraterrestrial visitors – beings from outer space.

# Answer: UNDECIDED

Some people believe that aliens from outer space crashed in Roswell, USA, in 1947. A rancher found unusual pieces of metal and other debris in his sheep pasture. He called the sheriff. The sheriff called the US Air Force. The Air Force collected all the materials in the field. The Air Force published a report. It said the unusual items were from a weather balloon. Many people believe that this report is a lie. They think that an alien spaceship crashed in the rancher's field. There is no official proof that an alien crash happened.

In 1976, 61-year-old Robert Taylor claimed that he saw a spacecraft from outer space in the Dechmont woods in Scotland. He was walking along a forest trail when he saw the UFO. It hovered just above the forest floor. Taylor said that it made no sound.

In 1989, Linda Napolitano of New York, USA, claimed that she was taken by figures she called "greys". She said she saw them hover outside her window. Other people claimed that they saw the incident happen just as Napolitano described.

 **IT'S TRUE!** Sometimes farmers discover strange formations called crop circles in their fields. Many crop circles have proven to have been made by people. But some people claim that other crop circles must have been made by aliens. No one knows for sure how some crop circles were created.

# CHAPTER 6

# THE FUTURE OF SPACE TRAVEL

Astronauts use remote manipulator systems, such as this one on the space shuttle *Discovery*, to increase safety.

Scientists study every planet in the solar system. They use telescopes on the ground and in orbit. They also use robotic spacecraft like the Mars rover *Curiosity*. Scientists collect important information about each planet. They want to understand more about the mysteries of space.

Many scientists say that crewed flights are not needed. Non-crewed flights are less expensive. They are also safer.

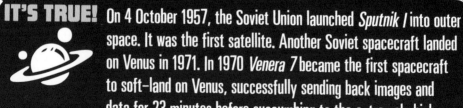

**IT'S TRUE!** On 4 October 1957, the Soviet Union launched *Sputnik I* into outer space. It was the first satellite. Another Soviet spacecraft landed on Venus in 1971. In 1970 *Venera 7* became the first spacecraft to soft-land on Venus, successfully sending back images and data for 23 minutes before succumbing to the extremely high temperature and pressure found on the planet's surface.

# Space programmes are now focused only on non-crewed missions.

## Evidence

Many space missions are successful. But some space missions end in tragedy. In 2011, NASA ended its space shuttle programme. Sending astronauts into space is expensive. Each crewed mission might cost as much as two or three non-crewed missions. Does this mean the end of crewed space travel?

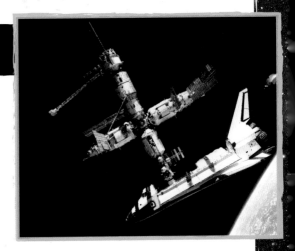

## Answer: UNDECIDED

Space programmes all over the world use crewed missions. They also use non-crewed missions. Many astronauts travel to the ISS. They do research while in orbit. Astronauts from Canada, Japan, Russia, the United States and 11 members of the European Space Agency send astronauts to the ISS. Several other countries have sent visitors to the ISS.

Non-crewed research missions are taking place throughout the solar system. The first successful non-crewed flight to Mars was in 1967. The most recent non-crewed mission launched in March 2016.

# FACT OR FIB?

## Regular people will soon be able to travel into space.

## Evidence

A private company called SpaceX launches rockets into the atmosphere. Then they land the rockets back on Earth. The spacecraft that shows the most promise is called Falcon 9.

## Answer: FACT

The Falcon 9 has successfully delivered a cargo capsule to the ISS. The capsule made it safely back to Earth with science samples. This means part of the rocket can be reused. This might make space travel less expensive and more accessible to average people.

Only part of SpaceX's Falcon 9 rocket lands back on Earth. It landed for the first time in 2015.

**IT'S TRUE!** SpaceX, the company that built Falcon 9, is working on building a spacecraft that can land on Mars.

# GLOSSARY

**asteroid** large space rock that moves around the sun

**astronomer** scientist who studies stars, planets and other objects in space

**atmosphere** layer of gases that surrounds some planets, dwarf planets and moons

**blackout** period of darkness caused by a power cut

**constellation** group of stars that appear to form a shape

**eclipse** when one object in space blocks light and stops it shining on another object in space

**Gregorian calendar** calendar used by much of the world; it was established in 1582 by Pope Gregory XIII

**International Space Station (ISS)** large spacecraft where astronauts live and work in space

**mass extinction** widespread and rapid decrease in life on Earth

**NASA** US government agency that does research on flight and space exploration; NASA stands for National Aeronautics and Space Administration

**orbit** path an object follows as it goes around the sun or a planet

**plasma** matter that is a collection of hot, charged atoms, such as those found in a fluorescent light bulb, neon sign or star

**rover** small vehicle that people can move by using a remote control; rovers are used to explore objects in space

**satellite** spacecraft that circles Earth; satellites gather and send information to Earth

**solar system** sun and the objects that move around it

**x-ray** powerful invisible rays that can pass through various objects

# FIND OUT MORE

## BOOKS

*Incredible Robots in Space* (Incredible Robots), Louise and Richard Spilsbury (Raintree, 2017)

*The International Space Station*, Clive Gifford (Wayland, 2017)

*Journey Into Space* (Planet Earth), Michael Bright (Wayland, 2016)

*Space Encyclopedia: A Tour of Our Solar System and Beyond*, David A Aguilar (National Geographic Kids, 2013)

## WEBSITES

**https://www.esa.int/esaKIDSen/SEMZXJWJD1E_LifeinSpace_0.html**
Learn more about the International Space Station.

**https://www.nasa.gov/kidsclub/index.html**
Find out how to be part of the NASA Kids' Club.

**https://solarsystem.nasa.gov**
Learn more about NASA's solar system exploration.

# INDEX